Crazy Good
Poems and perspectives on mental health.

By
Lauren Gann

I dedicate this book to my family. Thank you for being there for me in the darkest of times and never giving up hope. I will conquer this.

@I_am_crazygood

Table of Contents

Preface 1

Chapter 1 Dare To Dream 4

Chapter Two: This Mania Has a Hold of Me 13

Chapter three: Be a Survivor 29

Chapter Four: Medi-SIN or Medicine? 40

Chapter Five: Define It With Grace 50

Chapter Six: I Am Crazy Good. 60

Bibliography: 68

Abundance is EVERYWHERE — The energy you give is everything.... Vibe on!

PREFACE

For those of you who don't know me, in 2009, I was medicalized into the healthcare business. I was diagnosed with a chronic disorder with a very bleak prognosis. A disorder that doesn't just hurt you but hurts your loved ones - which hurts you more. A diagnosis that acts as a predefined cage of expectations leading to isolation due to its misunderstood nature and stigma. I chose the difficult path to healing. The path to befriend fear, sit with anguish, and taste the judgments, which meant doing this alone. My vocabulary and understanding of the English language are incapable of documenting the darkness that has enveloped me for more than a decade. Even if it could, I wouldn't want anyone to have any visibility of that darkness. It was my darkness, and I pledged not to spread it through empathy of others, for empathy is the duplication of emotion in another, which grows the darkness itself. I will not produce more darkness in this world. When it's that dark, a thunderstorm seems bright, for at least there are flashes of lightning. My previous statement seems dark and maybe self-loathing, but I assure you… that is the silver lighting - any light brings me comfort because I know it's better than lack of light. My power is my undeniable comfort due to this silver lining … in situations where most people are uncomfortable.

Fear is not a foe. Fear is my friend. Not the kind of friend you chose. But the one you must befriend because you can't escape them. My power also comes from this forced bravery. My mental and physical limitations are unshackled from fear. I understand deeply that these two combined side effects of my trauma/medicalization - no fear and no need for comfort - are my power. I pledge to use this power only to help heal the unhealed, to give hope when there is no hope, and to give perspective to catalyze one's activation of their own inherent power. Therefore, I write. Therefore, I listen. Therefore, I don't judge. Therefore, I am the way I am.

I had just landed. My mom was sitting to my left. I was sitting in the seat closest to the window, my favorite place to sit when I travel. But this wasn't a normal day. I wasn't my normal self. The pilot had asked us to pull the window shades down during descent due to the heat. I sat there, listening to the pilot instruct the passengers on the next steps to deplane, in Phoenix, AZ. I felt the heat from the window. I knew all too well that my destiny was not to deplane. I knew something that the others did not know. I knew what was on the other side of that plane door – **Hell**. I didn't care that the other passengers were going to Hell… they maybe deserved it, but me and my mom… that was not our destiny.

These were the delusions and hallucinations that were going around in my mind as I felt the heat of the Arizona summer on the plane window. Soon after, several police officers forcefully deplaned me. These hallucinations did not come out of nowhere; they arose from months of an untreated psychiatric disorder called Bipolar (I) disorder (formerly known as manic-depressive disorder). This was just one of the climaxes of the hallucinations that took me to another reality.

The funny thing about telling doctors this story is that they usually reply with "Phoenix in the summer is Hell" with a chuckle or two. They also proceed to ask me what illegal drugs I was taking, expecting cocaine, amphetamines, or hallucinogens. I was 20 at the time, and I had never done these types of drugs. I was an ex-college swimmer and chemistry student who had just submitted my first manuscript for publication. I was a daughter, the youngest of 3 siblings, and the girlfriend of my high school sweetheart. I had a track record for athletics and academics... never in my wildest dreams did anyone, including me, believe that I could have a mental disorder. Reality Check: I do have a mental disorder. I have Bipolar I disorder, and at 20, it was the average onset of symptoms – per the medical literature. The problem is that no one around me knew about bipolar disorder, including myself. That is something I am here to change. I want the diagnosis to help the healing. I am destined to make CrAzY.... CrAzY GOOD. Crazy good, to me, is being your best self as often as possible when you have a mental disorder. It is fighting daily for stability. It is getting up when you have been beat down. It is giving yourself grace to move forward – it is surviving. It is trusting your support network and your doctors/therapists. You will see my passion in words throughout the book. These poems have been my way of channeling my positive and negative emotions to make my crazy, crazy good. My hope is that others can proclaim, "I am crazy good" - Hope you enjoy the book!

CHAPTER 1
DARE TO DREAM

"Uninhibited Dreams" (2017)
When I was 17
I had a dream
That I deem
With high esteem.
Today I think I am fine,
But I cannot find
The state of mind
To produce dreams of those kind.

When I was young, I could do anything. I could dream uninhibitedly. I was an A student, graduated top of my class, played soccer on two teams, competed in Varsity track and Varsity Swimming. Anything I set my mind to, I accomplished. This ability to dream uninhibitedly as a young adolescent was my identity. I was strong, smart, fearless. Something changed when I was diagnosed with bipolar disorder because I began considering my identity as "broken" or diseased. This broken identity has kept me from dreaming uninhibitedly which decreased my quality of life. It's important to dream as uninhibitedly as possible as it constructs the vision of your life, and thus the execution of your life. The more limits you impose on your dreams, the more limitations you will have in your life. You cannot accomplish that which you cannot dream of or visualize. Because of my diagnosis, I created limitations on my life that affected me greatly. When I celebrated my 30th birthday it was a surprise to me because I could not picture myself surviving to turn 30 years old. I was incapable of not just dreaming for amazing things, but I couldn't even dream about surviving.

I lost the daydreamer in me for years after my diagnosis; one of the most detrimental aspects of the bipolar diagnosis in my opinion – It kept me from dreaming for better things to come and affected my quality of life. I lost it because I lost my identity and redefined myself as "broken". I felt unworthy of someone who wasn't broken. I felt like a burden on family and friends. I would date down. I would sell myself short, I would lower my standards. I would feel very differently about decisions and people depending on my mood. I felt like I had two personalities – neither of which was really me. I learned that you are not your emotions, but you are the sum of all your emotions because this is how you experience the world; they don't define you, but they do impact your reality. A great impact. That is why it is such a hard disorder. Your experience of reality is unstable at times. Thus, so is your life. Crazy Good's foundation is accepting your disability and the treatment, trusting the doctors and your support network, providing yourself grace to get back up, and never losing hope for tomorrow by keeping a dream of your life close to your heart; all in the name of being your best self – as often as possible. The best way to stay out of the hospital is to care for yourself with medications, a consistent sleep schedule, a routine, and meditation if possible.

"Scattered Identity" (2017)
I am in a competition
Full of repetition.
I compete with my emotions.
I even take crazy "potions".
I can't trust myself with these fluctuations,
I remember all too well my past hallucinations
But the fight is against LDG
Take a moment to see,
Emotions are a part of me.
I wonder what others think

But I can barely even drink
Down these pills.
In the mirror, I am still
Who am I?
What if I die?
I am LDG
I love honesty
I crave adventures
I hope to never have Dentures.
If I die,
I will leave my emotional legacy behind.
Maybe then someone will realize
That emotions are our experiences.

I remember a simpler time when I was on my high school swim team. Swimming miles a day for practice, I had finally made it to regionals and was placed 16th out of 16 with a time of 25.88 seconds in my 50-meter free; I barely made it. I recall being so excited to progress to regionals, I asked my coach, "So you are going to letter me now, right?" Note that getting a letterman jacket was the utmost prestige in my high school. He replied, "No, you need to make it to state." This meant I had to place in the top 3 at regionals. This is when I took the advice of my motivational video and "Dared to dream". I grabbed my water, went into the women's bathroom for some quiet time to do just that – DREAM. I had looked at the time sheets beforehand and I estimated that if I dropped 1 second on my time, I might have a chance. In that restroom, I visualized, uninhibitedly, "24.88" on the time board. I didn't think about the odds against me. I didn't think about the insane feat it would be to drop a second in a 50-meter freestyle. I dared to dream about getting a letterman jacket and making it to state – dropping a second was a nonnegotiable aspect of getting that jacket. At that moment, sitting in that restroom, I aligned every atom in my body towards the very daring goal of dropping a second on a 50 free. There was no dissonance in me to keep me from this goal. I had two races total to get me to my 24.88 – Prelims and Finals. I ended up going into finals in 8th place – barely making the cut. When it was time for the Finals, I sat in the "Ready Room" and put my goggles on… I heard the music play and the announcer say, "Lauren Gann from Klein High School in Lane 7". It was time to make my dream a reality. The race started and ended in a blur – I hit the touchpad and looked to the side and saw my entire team celebrating. I didn't have to see the clock; I could feel it in my being – 24.88!! I wore my letterman jacket with pride for the next 2 years.

    I highlight this pre-diagnosis success because it's the most discreet success I have ever achieved, and it highlights the power of daring to dream and visualization. I achieved this feat because I was unable to see that the odds were against me, to the point that I believed in myself more than ever. To me, I call it, "daring to dream". With my bipolar I diagnosis in 2009, daring to dream became a mirage for me. All I could fixate on were the limitations imposed by my diagnosis. I would try to tap into my dreams, but they wouldn't come to life like before. I remember my ability to visualize and execute effortlessly as an adolescent - while struggling to see a positive image of myself in my late 20s. All I could think about was the uphill battle. I think it had to do with the fact that the prognosis was devastating. Browsing the internet and talking with my doctors, these facts devastated me: "You have to take these medications for the rest of your life", "One in five people with your diagnosis commit suicide (1)", "Sometimes a [Bipolar I] success is just getting out of bed that day". I learned that you cannot let anything keep you from dreaming. It takes bravery to dream big – be brave. If Martin Luther King didn't dream about a better world for his race, would it have happened? If Elon Musk didn't dream about life on Mars, would he have started SpaceX? Daring to dream is the first step in every notable accomplishment. You dare to dream it; you dream it some more; you make an action plan to get it, and then you execute to accomplish it. All while using your dream as a compass to keep destructive energies/distractions at bay. I write to you today as I dare to dream – dare to dream of a world where we can make CrAzY, CrAzY good! A world where asking for help is okay, emotions are understood, and most importantly, the diagnosis helps the healing. A world where patients with a mental health disability are treated with compassion. I dare to dream today to show you it's possible; to remove mental blockages from your thinking if you have been diagnosed with bipolar disorder. I have been living my life since 2009 in the backseat of my own car on a journey with no path except the one behind me. This had to stop now, and I want to share with you all my story so you can also begin to dare to dream and live a crazy good life.

There is nothing more powerful than the human will when you can align all your atoms to one cause. The difficult part is determining that cause for alignment – that's where you need to be brave and DARE to DREAM! Dreaming is so important because this is your "why"; this is the reason you want to sacrifice the now for a better tomorrow. This is the progress that you need to bring you closer to happiness. This is the reason that you will persevere through the rough times and come out ahead. It is the vision of your life, the concept you desire the most, the alignment of your atoms. When I say dare to dream, I am not saying dare to dream about having a six-figure job, or to own a new car or house. I won't tell you to create a dream board from magazine cutouts full of advertisements and commercial goods/propaganda. I am not talking about consumer-based goals. I want you to dream about something that makes you emotional just thinking about it.

I want you to think big. So big, you feel uneasy about it at first. This dream, your why, should be something you can align your atoms towards. Something that you can make into a necessity of your existence, like the food you eat, the water you drink, and the shelter you seek. Your dream needs to closely tie in with the legacy and impact you want to drive during your short time on this planet. You need to be honest with yourself and understand what you want others to say about you while you are alive, and after you die. What will your obituary article say? What would you want it to say?

    When life was simpler for me, my goal was simple and discreet: to get a letterman jacket for swimming. Now, my dream is to change the lives and perspectives of those with bipolar disorder by leading by example – being Crazy Good. My dream is to conquer my illness not to the degree that I live a better life, but that it's so contagious that other people feel inspired to be able to conquer their own. I know that conquering my illness will be a daily battle – not one that occurs once.

    When your moods shift, you can feel like a different person. Your decisions are different, your interests are different, you are a different person. The reality is: you are not. The reality is you are a complicated integral of your emotions and moods because your emotions are how you experience the world. You need to find a dream that you can channel your emotions to; a dream you can channel yourself to. Align every atom in your being with this dream. So that no matter what emotion you are feeling, you can think of this dream, this "why", and realign your atoms. When you "fall off the horse" you need your dream and maybe a medical intervention to get you back on track. Sometimes it's like learning to live again – to take care of yourself, to do the necessary tasks to live a normal life. The first shower after a week of avoiding hygiene can feel like the first step after being paralyzed. The best things in life only became possible because someone dreamed it. My dream is to be the bipolar story that inspires others to give themselves grace for a better tomorrow and to live a crazy good life - daily.

> ***"Unwritten but not unthought" (2021)***
> *My dream creating a thought "circuit"*
> *But my pen waiting for the right time to insert it.*
> *The time is now, I am confident.*
> *I have conquered this fear of disappointment*
> *Hence, I am Unwritten.*
> *It's the word*
> *That I see in my proverb.*
> *I now remember,*
> *I can do anything; I need not confer.*

While there are many negative aspects of my diagnosis, I like to look for the silver lining. I am grateful for this diagnosis for many reasons. First, I am happy it happened to me and not to my brother/sister/loved one because I would rather go through it than see my family struggle like I did. I recall my first journal after my diagnosis. I just wrote, "Thank you that this happened to me." Bipolar disorder is a difficult thing to manage, but I felt confident that I was equipped to manage it and would rather be the person afflicted by this disorder than watch my family through it. I have always clung to the thought that I have the control and the power to conquer this illness; if it happened to my brother, I wouldn't have this full control.

While I didn't fully know I was bipolar, I knew something wasn't right months before my first manic episode. I just didn't know what it was. I recall looking back on my last journal writing during my manic episode, and it says in insane scribbles, "I think I am bipolar." I don't even remember writing that in my manic phase, but I knew something was not right. The diagnosis gave me security, knowing I was going to get help; little did I know the nonlinear journey I was embarking on. The diagnosis drove me to get the medications I needed. I am grateful that some of the most brilliant minds have dedicated their lives to studying bipolar disorder and have developed treatment for this difficult disorder – a couple decades ago, there were limited treatments available.

Another bittersweet reason I am grateful for my first manic episode and diagnosis is that it showed me who my "ride-or-die" support network was. I lost a lot of "friends", but in the end, the one who stayed during the worst, I cherish. I am lucky to have these people in my life through these intense times. I feel that you don't need to have a huge support network, just a couple of good people. The key is that you need to be able to trust these people with your life/mind – something that can be difficult to find. I am blessed to say that my family is my strongest support network, and I thank them for never losing hope in me, even in the darkest of times.

In addition, I feel like I, when my symptoms are managed, am happier than the average American because I have a team of professionals (therapists and doctors) who are dedicated to maximizing my happiness, and I make a conscious effort to be as happy and stable as possible. I have studied the art of happiness, what brings happiness, and I am taking medications to help with happiness. This is because if I am not happy, the negative emotions I feel are so strong that they can be destructive and self-deprecating. I cannot afford to be in a destructive state of mind because statistics show that it kills. I have made my happiness and journey toward happiness a priority because I don't just want to be happy; my survival depends on my happiness. Having the concept of happiness and positive emotions at the forefront of my mind makes me feel like I am ahead of many Americans. My dad always told me the goal of life is to be happy. I take this to heart and I know that I can't always be happy due to reality and chemical imbalances, but I know I am doing my best to achieve the goal of happiness with the help of professionals. This prioritization of happiness would not be so defined in my life had it not been for my diagnosis.

Lastly, it has been shown that there is a trend between bipolar patients and creativity/art. I was analytically driven my entire life, but when I read about this trend and became more introspective, I realized that I am creative. I connect dots that others don't, and I am proud of my mind for that. My thought patterns are sometimes erratic and destructive, but they are also unique and creative. This is how I got into writing poems with no formal training. I liked Eminem growing up and just started "making rhymes to activate your minds". Being creative is an important trait nowadays, given the current technological trends of Artificial Intelligence taking over routine jobs and tasks; being creative is marketable! I think that there is a strong correlation between madness and genius, between insanity and creation. I am fascinated by the concept that I could create a unique creative idea to change the world; my mind is structured for this creation! I think outside the box, and in my heart, I know that a **good** idea never dies.

I realize that my stability depends on my actions. My future depends on my stability. I realize that I need to be happy and that I deserve to be happy – just like every other person. My brain is special, my dream is important. By clinical standards, I am different than most people. I can feel more, dream more! It may be **my** crazy idea that impacts the world. I resonate with Aristotle when he said, "There is no great genius without a mixture of madness." We, the mentally ill, just need to keep the "madness" at bay, and we **can** with modern medicine and support.

"Mechanical Thoughts" (2020)
Our cosmos are dimensions,

Coexisting in the ether that connects-us
Waiting to be organized by thought.
A thought,
It's all you've got!
A thrill only last "until"…
But an idea never dies.
It only grows in size.
My intuition
Tells me no
To repetition.
My mind
Tells me yes
To one of a kind.
I love novelty
I hold it custody
It keeps me out of poverty.
You see…
Newness grows dendrites
Making you go to new heights.
While routine…
Makes you a machine.
Stay Keen,
Create.
Stay Unforeseen;
Don't be a machine.

CHAPTER TWO:
THIS MANIA HAS A HOLD OF ME

"Collective Consciousness" (2019)
You see,
Emotions are my domain…

*I have felt the darkest pain…
But from this, there was gain.*

*It's August 3rd, 2009,
Yeah, I am out of my mind.
Scared,
I find the kind of hell
You cannot foretell.
A kind of pain
That leaves a stain
On your calendar day:
One year.
Two year.
Three year…. Four
Did pretty well, I couldn't get past that score!*

*It's July 3rd, 2014.
When I became "un-freed" by authorities
Because of the need for society
To label me
And predict my density.
I sang, yes, I SHOUTED…. but my screams were never heard.
It was 16 days, 16 nights; my name: stigmatized
My mind: compromised.
My privacy: nullified.
Was told I was "gravely disabled"
Sitting in an ER hallway for 9 hours…
I wish this was a fable.
Don't worry, nowadays I'm stable….
I understand that life is like a cycle for me,
Mother Nature's destiny
They call it Bipolar I in formality,
Unable to understand the dichotomy –
Up, Down,
Smile, Frown*

I am bound
For greatness, LOOK AROUND.

"Crazy" is in,
Stop thinking it's a sin.
It's a revolution in evolution
And should not force us to create a societal occlusion.

Realize that normal is the enemy of creation,
When looking for a new solution,
We want that evolutionary mutation.
The idea that changes everyone's fixation…

"Normal" people don't understand
That mental illness in society expands
Our whole consciousness –
Helping problem-solving reconnaissance!

I have realized that mistakes are beneficial,
They look like failures
But REEK of potential…
Learning curves and mishaps are essential…
For breaking out of the conventional.

This is because: "misguided" neural pathways, allow us to create…
The word "Illness" denotes hate,
Rather, let's embrace the face of 'disgrace'
Let's make mental stigma an enigma.
Let's empower those with this evolutionary super-power

You see,
Emotions are my domain…
I have felt the darkest pain…
But from this, there is gain.

I basked in chaos and found a unique perspective,
From this, I will continue to help the collective.

Bipolar I disorder is characterized by mania and depression. Everyone is technically "bipolar"; everyone experiences positive poles/emotions and negative poles/emotions. To be clinically diagnosed as Bipolar, your range of emotions is larger than the average person, and this fact affects your quality of life and activities of daily living (ADLs). The ADLs, such as cleaning your house, brushing your teeth, eating, showering, and doing laundry, can be affected by a clinically diagnosed bipolar patient's manic or depressive episodes to the point of disability. While suffering from an episode, you may be so euphoric you forget to eat, or you could be so depressed you don't want to shower. In fact, the American Disability Act has classified bipolar disorder as a disability. You may hear people calling their girlfriends or themselves bipolar; many times, people use this word not as a clinical diagnosis but more of a descriptive term. This can be hurtful to people with bipolar because we know the debilitating aspects of the disorder. I wish this term could only be used as a diagnosis. This can only happen with education and awareness for the disorder.

In modern psychiatry, they compare being bipolar to being diabetic. I think they do this to **try** to ease patient's minds about their bipolar prognosis, highlighting that it can be managed with medication. I have always had a problem with this analogy because it simplifies the relationship between your mood and your treatment. A diabetic person doesn't wake up one day and decide not to take their medication because of their mood. Missing insulin doesn't make you more likely to miss your next insulin dose. Insulin doesn't just stop working because of environmental factors like psychiatric medications. Bipolar is very complicated because it interferes with your mind, that which governs all your actions and decisions. Regulating your moods with medication works, but only if your mood and decision making is stable enough to keep you compliant with your medication. External factors you cannot control affect your mood/disorder like a death of a family member, a loss of a job, or a divorce. In addition, there are no biomarkers for Bipolar. In diabetes, you take a test, and you find out you need insulin. For mental diagnoses, they ask you a couple of subjective questions. Sometimes, the questions seem circular. They ask if you have been hallucinating or seeing things others have not been seeing. My reply is, how would I know? I live in my reality, and hallucinations are my reality at times. I don't know what others see or don't see. Another question asked revolves around sleep: How many hours have you been sleeping? Seems like a simple question, but when I am deep in psychosis, I don't know how to answer this question. I don't require sleep like I normally do when I am this manic, and my reality is blurred between the sleep state and the awake state – which is terrifying. Diagnosing and treating psychiatric disorders is difficult because it relies on a narrative from a potentially sick patient to get help instead of a biomarker. Some characteristics of mania may be totally normal for some, like being goal oriented. That is why you must have a baseline of what is normal for you to get a proper diagnosis. Given the range of quality in medical doctors, there are many misdiagnoses. Heck! I was diagnosed with PMDD, but I ended up being bipolar. My friend has been diagnosed as schizophrenic for years, but just got a bipolar diagnosis. In addition, being prescribed the wrong medication can exacerbate or generate psychotic symptoms; many people are diagnosed with unipolar depression end up having bipolar - the SSRI medications they are prescribed for depression may at times trigger a manic episode. Also, there are no studies to determine the acute and longitudinal effects of going off of psychiatric medications. No pharmaceutical company is going to pay for these studies. They do not want you to stop the medications. Sometimes, the withdrawals can be awful. If stopped too quickly, it can trigger an episode. You can find blogs and forums online of patients that are taking up to 5 medications daily for their bipolar disorder. These people give bone-chilling stories for the effects they have experienced by tapering off the meds – even when it's been supervised by the medical doctor. Many indicate that they do not have the ability to describe what they are experiencing, which includes out-of-body experiences.

    I think what is most difficult about bipolar disorder as a disability is that it's episodic. You would not deny that someone in a wheelchair needs extra assistance to live their lives, but with mental disorders, it isn't always evident, and we can be functional... sometimes. You don't know that I have been in bed unable to function the past three days because you only saw me for 20 minutes the day I was feeling better. There are reasons why an episodic disability can be difficult for the average person to understand. This is because the mind wants things to be as consistent as possible. This is the reason McDonald's is so successful. They provide the same experience and taste repeatedly and consistently. The mind likes going to McDonald's and knowing the product is predictable. Conversely, if you have a restaurant that sometimes has good-tasting food but sometimes doesn't, you will probably think twice about going there because there is a risk that they won't have good-tasting food. Analogously, people like people that stay in character. People like people that are consistent because inconsistency can pose a threat to them. It's evolutionary and ingrained in people. This is what makes bipolar disorder so difficult; you can't see it, and when you do see it, it comes up as a character inconsistency or episodically. It's also not physical – patients still look healthy **most** of the time. I hope that one day we can look at bipolar patients just like other disabilities, that patients just need a little extra assistance to function. We will get there but reducing stigma and getting help for those that need it comes first. I believe it starts with being vulnerable and open with people you can trust about your struggles. If no one knows what you stuggle with, how can they help you? It can be difficult to find people to trust, but there are many support networks available through non-profit organizations that could help.

Most women struggle with the depression side of bipolar disorder. Men are typically the ones who struggle with the mania. I have had my depressive moments, but those episodes don't have anniversaries like my three manic episodes. Manic episodes leave a stain on your calendar day; you think of them every year. Let me explain some aspects of my episodes and some of the debilitating emotions I was left with. My first episode was intense and included five cities, four worried family members, three months, two arrests/mental hospitals, one diagnosis. I was doing summer research for Trinity University Chemistry Department as part of my undergraduate degree. I was on the path to contribute to the medical discourse by becoming a doctor, and I felt like my bipolar diagnosis turned the medical society (something I aspired to be a part of) against me; thus, I felt that something I felt aligned with, turned on me. I lived alone in my first apartment during this summer, I worked in the lab, went to parties, studied for the GRE/MCAT, and stopped sleeping. I lost 50 lbs. Mania had gradually begun. Mania doesn't just hit you overnight; it builds; and it mostly occurs during the summer months. Unknowingly, I had created the perfect recipe for mania. The difficult part is that it feels good. Imagine if someone told you that you are "too happy", you have "too much energy". No one will say this unless they are aware of mental disorders; they will celebrate your manic achievements. The best way I can describe mania is Mario

Kart's Star Power and it can evolve into a God-like grandiosity. Pre-psychosis, unfortunately others celebrated my mental state, because no one in my life knew that mental illness could be a factor. I lost weight – celebrated, I worked extensive hours – celebrated, I lost my filter – people thought I was hilarious. If there were people that noticed that my personality was shifting and my mind was slipping, I could have avoided the intense psychosis that followed in the coming months. It is most important to have people that see you every day and know your personality to help identify the health of your mind – I was missing this as I was living alone. Mania is a series of chemicals/neurotransmitters being released into your brain. It starts gradually, and then you have intense epiphanies about life and other problems you have been thinking about. Suddenly, everything feels easy. It feels amazing – until you have climbed the cliff too high that you fall off the other side – into paranoia and psychosis. Unfortunately, my paranoia and psychosis started when my summer vacation began. I was with a friend at her family's vacation in Hilton Head, North Carolina, when my delusions and psychosis kicked in full swing. My friend's family called my family and let them know I was "acting funny". They put me on a plane back home; my parents said it was probably stress. This is the start of one of the most traumatic experiences of my life.

When I talked with my doctors after the next month or so, I talked with little confidence about the events that occurred. The doctor indicated that when your mind and body go through something as traumatic as I went through, your mind forgets it to protect you; the things I remember are more delusions than reality. I got arrested in the airport (and taken to a mental hospital) of Charlotte during my layover from Hilton Head. I don't recall what I was doing, to be honest, but I remember just wanting to be home and having everyone keep me from getting home. I was cavity searched at the hospital and had an injection into my right buttock, probably Ativan. I only know these things happened because I had handprint bruises on my shoulders and a huge knot on my buttock for weeks to come. *Somehow*, my mom arrived at the mental hospital in Charlotte. She is a superhero. We had a consultation with the doctor, where he indicated that I am bipolar and that I need to take these medications (he handed my mom an envelope with a couple of doses of pills). My mom and I ventured off to the Charlotte airport where we had a layover in Phoenix, Arizona.

    I remember my mom giving me the medications as prescribed by the doctor, but I was paranoid. I felt that if I took the medications, I was going to die. So, I pretended to take the meds and left them in the bathroom. We got on the airplane, and my delusions started to get very scary. I looked outside the window and saw about 100 airplanes all being drawn to the same place we were going. I somehow knew what had occurred: the apocalypse had come – there was now a portal to hell on earth, and the devil was taking fleets of planes (including mine) to this portal.

    There are many forums and comments about mania being a type of spiritual awakening. It sure does feel that way when you have reached mania, but I firmly believe it is simply an inbalance of neurotransmitters. Grandiosity has been documented as a symptom of bipolar disorder frequently and consistently. When I had my manic episodes I had many religious hallucinations about God and the Devil. I felt I could control things out of my control and that I was divinely protected and invincible. If you start feeling this way, that is a sure sign you need to talk with a doctor. Do not confuse sprituntuality and religion for a manic episode – it can be tragic.

    Now imagine this, I have always trusted my brain, I have always had good outcomes trusting my brain, and now I know I am in danger and so is my mom. The plane lands,

I feel the heat on the window. It confirms we have landed in the portal of hell. I am positive that if we wait it out, the plane will leave, and my mom and I could avoid going to hell. I stand my emaciated ground at 100 pounds and declare I will not be getting off the plane. My dad calls, and I break my mom's phone in half! I am in a fearful, manic, and in a surreal state. Imagine having a realistic dream where you were out of character and crazy things were happening…just to find out you were awake and it wasn't a dream. The authorities come and forcefully remove me and handcuff me. I was fighting to stay on the plane and remember the moment when they detained me by force – I was like a scared kitten that finally met its match. My brother and I chatted, and he is certain that if he was in my situation, they would have used much more brute force against him; I am lucky I was a 100 pounds and a female. I think overall they did the best they could, but this was the first instance that caused severe trauma for the police.

After being deplaned, the delusions didn't stop. While I am in route to another mental facility, I have a manic epiphany – I am in hell now, and it seems like normal life – "WOW! Hell isn't so bad!" At this point, my father drives from San Diego to pick me and my mom up from Phoenix. I am ever so grateful for my support network and their all-hands approach to protect me. I remember sleeping in the back of the car on the way to my parents' home in San Diego– sleep being something I had not done in a while. In the next coming months, I was prescribed Depakote and Zyprexa; I gained 60 pounds in a month and was sleeping about 16 hours a day. I am ever so grateful for my doctor, Dr. Katz, who was able to get my mind back. Realistically, I should have been in an inpatient ward, but I think my mind came back due to the comforts and support I received. I remember still having delusions and psychosis during the time I was at home recovering. I am thankful for how the recovery went, as there are patients that don't bounce back like I did. The doctor anticipated it would be 6 months before I would return to my normal behavior – it was more like 2 months. I returned to San Antonio in time for my birthday at the end of October, but I was taking the semester off school given the medical situation. This was the start of the darkest depression I have ever experienced; what goes up, must come down. I struggled with the fact I had to take medication, I felt awkward that I couldn't drink alcohol like others in college, I struggled with the side effects, I didn't fully accept my diagnosis, and I felt shame, fear, and worst of all, I was having an identity crisis. I felt no one understood me, my boyfriend of 5 years broke up with me, I wasn't swimming anymore, and my 2 roommates/"best friends" unsuccessfully tried to get me off our lease. You don't know who your support network is until you need support. That is for sure.

    I changed medications, changed doctors, and even tried herbal remedies for a while until in 2014 when I decided to go off my medication, which resulted in another manic episode. To give you an idea, I have been on 11 different psych medications, and I have seen about 8 different doctors. I had been told that I caused myself to be bipolar due to occasionally smoking cannabis, I had been triggered to have suicidal thoughts through the medications, I had felt out-of-body experiences from the medications. I had a doctor prescribe an SSRI (Lexapro) which is contraindicated for my disorder and then he proceeded to go into administrative work shortly after. This led to manic symptoms and horrid withdrawals from getting off the SSRI. All of this while trying to live a "normal" life with a job, aspirations, and dating. Going off medication is a typical mistake that many people with my diagnosis make. It's a complex issue that is personal for every patient; and it is complicated by the "Star Power" feeling you get with mania (which is stunted inherently with the medications). The difference between this episode and my last was, my support network knew I was bipolar which decreased the impact of the episode because I was able to get help sooner, even if it was against my desires at the time – I am grateful it happened now.

This time when I was taken to a mental institute by the police, I was held on a 5150 (72-hour hold) against my will on 4th of July weekend. I was angry, I was lucid, and I was manic. I was so upset I decided to show these people what crazy really was (maybe not the best idea). They had me in an ER hallway bed for several hours where I started singing the national anthem from the top of my lungs. I felt that my freedom was taken away because of my diagnosis on America's birthday. This irony was why I decided to sing and shout. I didn't really think I was manic at the time, but in hindsight, I was sick. I was the worst patient; I refused help and medications during my 5150. They extended the 5150 to 5250 (15 Day hold). I ended up being in the mental institute for 16 days. Twice I was chemically restrained, and I was also interviewed by the medical director of the academic facility. That interview still infuriates me because the doctor paraded me around while I was angry to all the residents. I went to court against my doctor and lost – it became legal for the academic hospital to treat me without consent. I was beyond angry at the world, locked up with no comforts of home, surrounded by strangers that were also psychotic and struggling, and being watched and judged constantly by technicians who are required by law to monitor you and take notes on your behavior every 15 minutes. I started complying with medication PO (by mouth) because I came to terms after court that I had no other option. I started to balance out and was released two days early from my hold.

I met the most interesting people during my 16-day stay. Many of them were like me, many of them not like me. From an oxycodone addict who was upset about the hospital taking his prescription away, to schizophrenics who were difficult to understand, to the 300-pound lady who would run around the ward naked. We were all there for different reasons, different types of suffering, but we all had one thing in common – we needed help. The healthcare system attempts to help us, but it falls short as there is a cycle or discharge and readmittance. Also, they pride themselves on not using restraints, but they have just replaced the physical restraints with chemical restraints. I recall being put into a room, being injected, and waking up in my bed the next day not knowing what happened. The entire hospitalization process is very traumatic; if you weren't crazy before, you will be crazy during hospitalization. Imagine your doctor doing rounds on you and looking at you for 30 seconds, writing some notes, and walking away. He is the only person that can free you from an involuntary hold, and he won't even give you more than a minute of his time. Also, when you get admitted, they take all your comforts away. You will undergo caffeine withdrawals. Some places don't let you smoke cigarettes, many times your clothes are compromised, and you must eat terrible food.

During my third manic episode, I witnessed, in my 17 days, one patient be hospitalized in the same unit three times and another twice. One of the most difficult aspects of staying healthy for mentally ill patients is that 1) patients become married to the healthcare system and are expected to be medicated and supervised by a medical professional for the rest of their lives; 2) the medication and professionals are very expensive 3) insurance can be out of reach and not very helpful with needed medication treatment – this is why I went without insurance when I quit my job and lost mine. Now I know that there are local programs that help patients without insurance and a job, but if you don't know about these services, they are useless. I recommend learning about what services are in your area in the event you need access to your medication and struggle financially. It's never a smart idea to stop medication – there are programs out there to help.

    My most recent manic episode kept me hospitalized for 17 days. I walked into the Emergency room, paranoid and delusional, because I didn't have insurance and didn't know where to go. They discharged me home, and with the help of my support network, I tried outpatient medication. It did not work, and my condition got worse. An ambulance took me back to the ER where 4 cops were called in the middle of the night. I was restrained and injected, and I was transferred to Cypress Creek hospital. I was very psychotic at this point, and I didn't know what was going on. The first couple of days I do not remember at all. My memory is a broken scene that just doesn't make sense. The only thing I had to show for my first days was the bruises on my body. I had handprints from the cops and an enormous bruise given to me by a technician in the hospital. The bruise was behind my knee and was larger than my palm. I submitted a complaint to the Joint Commission, but I was hurt in my room where no cameras were available – it was dismissed. When I did come back to reality, I was very angry. One day, I was very angry with the nurses, and this other patient grabbed me and asked me how to make a fortune teller from a sheet of paper. Another day, I was very angry at the therapists; the patient came over and asked me to go to group therapy with him. Almost every day, he would make sure I was going to the gym. Davion and I became friends. We colored together, we watched movies, we played music, we ate and shared lunch, we did origami, we did therapy and went to the gym, and we even played patty cake. A moment I will never forget was when I was sitting next to him in group therapy, and they asked everyone to say something nice about the person next to them. I was next to him, and he said he liked my personality. I think we have such a spiritual connection because we met with no expectations, little hope, and a bunch of planned-out activities. Cypress Creek provided an environment unlike any dating scene – it allowed me to be vulnerable and upfront with Davion – something that takes a while in modern dating. Davion and I were at very similar points in our lives, with very little going for us.

We were in the hospital together for 8 days total, spending 14 hours together on average. On the night before I was being discharged, my heart got heavy, thinking I would never see him again. I wrote him a note and folded it into a paper football. His roommate gave it to him the day I left. He would begin calling me from the hospital until he got discharged 4 days later.

The first day we met "in the free world," I was full of emotion. I saw him and fell in love. I met his mom when I walked into their house. She and I had already been texting. We ended up at a boba tea shop, and we had our first kiss. We continued seeing each other, got engaged, and moved in together in October.

Love is my purpose. I love love. I had an intense love-filled relationship with my high school sweetheart. He broke my heart when we broke up shortly after my diagnosis in 2009. Since the diagnosis, two themes arose in my heart regarding love: 1) I don't want to marry someone with mental illness 2) Anyone who would put up with me will suffice. I struggled deeply with accepting my diagnosis as manageable, so much that I could not image being in a relationship with someone else struggling– that would make a relationship impossible, I thought. I was judging myself, and this judgment bled into feeling bad for anyone who "got stuck" with me. Now I see it's because I was so insecure about my identity of being bipolar. This self-judgement, coupled with COVID loneliness led me to a terrible relationship, which contributed to my last manic episode. During this manic episode at Cypress Creek Hospital, I met a trusty companion, Davion.

What Davion has shown me is that everyone needs a little help sometimes. No one is perfect. He really understands my diagnosis and has seen me, and helped me, at my very worst. I feel that he cares for my feelings. We are now engaged. I am blown away by how much **better** it is to date someone with a mental illness. We keep each other healthy. We give each other grace. We remind ourselves about taking our meds. We ensure we are sleeping well. I feel safe around him even when I am triggered or angry and unreasonable. I have begun to think that those who have mental illness probably have a bigger heart because of Davion. When you have so much pain, and you can find someone who understands that and has been through that, it helps ease the pain. Davion and I are kindred spirits.

I hope this love story helps you love yourself more; don't judge yourself for your mental illness and have hope for love if you need it. Everyone deserves love, and sometimes you find it in unexpected places – sometimes in the most hopeless of situations.

The final bill for the two ER visits was $26,000, not including lab costs and physician costs. Thankfully, Tricounty paid for my inpatient visit, which was $42,000, and I was living at my parent's house at the time. This was just the financial impact for my hospitalization, let alone the reckless spending I underwent before the hospitalization. I was left with credit card and medical debt and little esteem to get a job. I was underwater and needed to rebuild. I have since gotten a job, moved into my apartment with Davion, paid off my medical and credit card debt, and been compliant with my medication and consults with doctors. I now take my medication religiously because I have made a pact to never to go back to an Inpatient Psych Ward again. Healthcare is broken, and we don't know how to care for people with mental disorders. That is why you must rely on your support network and yourself to manage your condition whenever possible. Taking medications and being compliant is a significant aspect of managing yourself outside of an inpatient facility; something that I learned the hard way.

One aspect that is difficult for me to deal with is the slow pace of life – or the perceived slow pace of life. During a manic episode you are very productive (or start many projects at least) and it seems like your dopamine receptors are saturated. Once you come down and stabilize, things can feel a little drab. Your mind is slower, you lose your "Star Power". This can be disheartening and a reason why many people don't like to be fully stable – it's just boring. I am working to live with less dopamine, a calmer and more stable life. It is difficult to accept a mind with less ideas and productivity, but it is something I am willing to accept in the name of stability. Life doesn't always have to be exciting is something I am learning.

CHAPTER THREE:
BE A SURVIVOR

"The walls are closing in" (2021)
Is there really a reason to live?
I am paralyzed by this emotion
I am irritated by any commotion.
It keeps me out of the present
It makes me hesitate
About my future
But I need to persevere
But for what?
Everyone else has their lives set up
And I cannot even get out of my funk.
Little things set me into a spiral

What are my triggers:
Lack of fullness.
I am angry
I am upset.
I can't help but repent
That fact that I am a waste of life
I feel like it's all been a lie.
Which is why I stand here
Wondering
Why
Do I assume
That life
Is something more than a sick confine.

Twenty percent of people with bipolar disorder self-destruct. This disorder is fatal to 1 in 5 people who are diagnosed. This is due to the bipolar depression and mixed episodes which can be very difficult to treat. I personally feel that bipolar depression is an intensified depression because it is juxtaposed or contrasted with mania. The drop is thus more intense.

It can be very difficult to achieve long term goals with bipolar disorder because you are consistently inconsistent – thus, you must be persistent. It's a cycle of feeling confident and stable, feeling unstoppable, and then feeling like there is no hope and that the world is a dark hole in the universe. Sometimes, the cycles can last a couple of days, weeks, or even months.

It is difficult for me to know what part of the cycle I am in while I am in it. All I can say is give yourself grace when you can pick yourself up. Don't think in terms of the past – pick up today. Conquer today. Today makes for tomorrow, yet tomorrow comes but never arrives. Use a journal to work through what happened to you when you were depressed or manic. Talk to a therapist regulary to get perspective on what you are going through. Give yourself grace, forgive yourself, and live in today. You will feel good, and then you will get knocked down; **always get back up**. This is about survival.

Life Wisdom (2015)
Today, I will change the world.
Tomorrow, the world will end.
Yesterday doesn't exist.

    Studies have shown that a routine can really help mood shifts. I have struggled, and I work on a routine every day. It's very difficult for me. Things that you can work putting into a routine, maybe incrementally, can be simple and will provide you benefits. The first routine activity you should manage is your medication compliance. Sometimes, external factors can affect this compliance. I struggled with morning doses because my medicine required there to be food in my stomach, and sometimes I didn't eat until 2 in the afternoon. If I took the medication without food, I would vomit in 20-30 minutes, getting to taste the nasty medication. I also used to struggle with a nighttime regimen because sometimes I would go to bed at 5:30 PM, while other times, 2 AM. These are some external factors that can affect medication compliance. A couple of days off your compliance routine can compound and keep you off your medication. A couple of days off your medication can make you feel better, depending on the side effects you are accustomed to living with. The second (or maybe tied for first) routine you should accomplish is your sleep routine. Go to sleep and wake up at the same time every day as often as possible. Go to sleep when the sun goes down, and the sun goes up if possible. Every cell in your body has a sensor for light. There is not a clear understanding, but there are studies that believe bipolar disorder is a disorder of the Circadian rhythm. I like to sleep with the blinds a little open to help me see the sun when it goes up and down, and I feel it helps. Another very important aspect of routine is diet. Not just what you eat, but when you eat it. Food, just like a drug, can change your mood. Some foods influence your mood more than others. The difference between eating broccoli or an ice cream. Being able to eat low fat, low-sugar, high-protein diet is very helpful in managing mood. You are free from the risk of a sugar crash; you have less hanger. Also, the timing seems to influence the predictability of moods. Try to eat at the same time every day. This can be either very easy or very difficult, depending on the rest of your schedule if you cannot eat at the same time every day, it's ok! It's more important to avoid sugar and very fatty foods! Try lean proteins and vegetables. It will help your body composition and your mood. I guarantee it.

Starting work at the same time of the day can also help. Starting your first human interaction at the same time of day will also affect your mood in a predictable way. If you can, work out; if you can work out at the same time of day. I talk to my mom every single morning as I make my coffee and take my meds. Everything you do affects your neurotransmitters. The time of day, how long you have been awake, if you have eaten – If you can control some of these stimuli, it will help you control your mood because all these stimuli cause shifts in mood. Again, it can be very difficult to have this tight of a routine. Try to start with meds and sleep. There are some concepts about habit-stacking that can also help when building a routine.

My worst depression was in 2009-2010 when I came down from my first manic episode. I can describe this depression as a cavity in my chest that was gradually caving in little by little. It was like my chest had a well inside of it, whose diameter would slowly increase minute after minute. I still think of this imagery, and it takes me back to the deep hopelessness I felt after my mania. I could literally feel the pressure on my chest. Not only was I coming down from mania, but I wouldn't be able to graduate with my class, and my 5-year relationship would come to an end. I had a promise ring he gave me that I lost in my episode. He bought me another just to break up with me 4 months later. One conflict we started having after my diagnosis was that I could not be happy. He was dedicated to being my partner and "making me happy". With my neurotransmitters coming down from euphoria, there was no way I could be "happy." This has been an ongoing insecurity for me because I am not always happy. I am sometimes hopeless or numb. It can be for a couple of days or for weeks. Thankfully, Dave was able to talk with me about my insecurities and reassure me that he will love me in all my moods. He cares about my feelings. Being ok with not being happy all the time is something I work on often.

 I survived bipolar disorder depression in 2009/2010 because of a quote I wrote that helped funnel the emotion I was experiencing: "life is the unsuccessful organization of chaos". To me, this quote let me feel ok to fail; ok to not organize and control – the ability to know that entropy and chaos were imminent (and thermodynamically favorable), so I wasn't alone in this feeling because it is what life is. I felt like life was built for failure, so my "failure" wasn't that bad.

 Depression and suicidal thoughts can come in different flavors. You can feel like you just want to disappear from the world and evaporate. Maybe you just want to sleep and never wake up. You can hope that someone drives their 18-wheeler into your car on the highway or that the bridge you are driving on collapses. You can be taking a bath and wonder if drowning would really be that bad. It can also be more acute and result in a plan or in self-harm. I have had different experiences of suicidal thoughts, but I have never had an attempt. I am too scared and feel it's a very selfish thing to do to my support network. Depression can also have different intensities. It can be the inability to get out of bed for days at a time, the apathy towards hygiene, or it can be the lack of light in your life. There have been moments for me when I walk outside and finally see the light in life, just to realize that I had been depressed the previous weeks. "People don't pretend to be depressed. People pretend to be ok" is the truest statement. Some of the happiest seeming people are depressed and have ended their lives, like Robin Williams. I think that people who experience depression tend to have a kinder heart than others because they empathize with emotional pain in others. Also, sometimes you don't even know you have been depressed until you aren't depressed anymore. It can be difficult to know what life is "supposed to" be like with regard to mood. There are mood tracking apps and recommendations to mood track from providers. This has been difficult for me to get behind without complete obsession. I started tracking my moods, and then all I could think about was my mood, not the moment. Also, once you have tracked them, how do you decide that you aren't happy enough? How do you know you need medical intervention for your functional depression? There is no formula and its normal to experience some mood shifts. This makes managing your mood difficult because it is not clear cut – it's subjective and looks different for everyone. That being said, tracking moods can be helpful because many times I have a terrible mood in the morning, but by evening I forgot I went through that emotional pain; I think it's the minds way to cope with the shifts in mood.

  When I first was recovering from my first manic episode, I was so afraid to have a happy day because I would question if I was about to go manic again. The best tool I have found is to journal. When you are happy, when you are sad, when you are angry; maybe it isn't even words. It's a doodle. Maybe it isn't events that occurred but a stream of consciousness you need to get out. The journaling can be good for getting emotions out of you, but I think the more valuable aspect of journaling is to go back and see your progress. I write in my journals often, and I will pick up an old journal and see what I was dealing with 5 years ago or last month. It helps me see my current state better and reminds me of what I have been through. There are many techniques for journaling out there. I have really enjoyed choosing a word and then attempting to rhyme to it while evoking my emotions. This is what has created my poetry in this book. Most poems were created while I was in complete tears, drenched in emotion, which is how it helped me process these deep emotions.

    I continue to be a Bipolar survivor due to several perspectives that have helped me ground myself. The first is that every emotion, good or bad, is temporary. This is especially true with bipolar disorder considering the emotions are caused by neurotransmitter imbalances. I also have created a pledge/pact system with myself where I pledge not to self-destruct. I will be above that statistic and will not let this happen. I have it written in my journal: "I pledge not to self-destruct" and I take that commitment very seriously. Do I have suicidal thoughts? Yes. Are they awful? Absolutely. But I paralyze my actions before any harm is done and reach out to my trusty doctors/professionals. I do this for my support network, my mom, my dad, my brother, and sister when I don't see the value in doing it for myself. I have found that it is very difficult to reach out to family members or people in your support network because they are not trained to handle these types of situations/thoughts – they could very easily say the wrong thing. I would, unless your support network is trained, leave it to your therapist and psychiatrist. If you are afraid that you cannot keep yourself safe, check yourself into an inpatient facility; there are people out there that can get you the help you need.

"A part of our bipolar fate" 2021
Depressed state –
It's part of our oppressed bipolar fate.
Oppressive self-hate...
I have this feeling to date.
The bipolar nation –
Totaling 2.3 million American faces
This depressive iteration
Of reality creates a complicated
Emotional compilation within us bipolar patients.
The juxtaposition of the two conditions (manic: depressive)
Makes survival less auspicious.
I don't have a good solution.
Depressed thoughts are pollution,
It's no collusion
That depression
KILLS!
I advise, take your pills
And to be paralyzed by this negative emotion
Don't over-analyze and act on your mental commotion.
Lean into the pain.
And in a temporary amount of time, it will refrain...
This is your bipolar journey: recall, you aren't completely sane!
Pause your actions
So, you don't regret your reactions.
Remember its ok to cry
And doing this will pry
Neurotransmitters
From your mind
That are causing this hellish confine
In your being.
Remember its ok to sleep,
Doing this will keep
your mind reconsolidating its chemicals....

And you will soon awake into a new kind of reality
Where you can find more positivity.

    The best antidote for a terrible emotion, in my opinion, is to cry and sleep it off. It sounds simple, and it is, but there is science behind it. Your tears drain chemicals out of your body. Sleep reconsolidates your experiences and reframes your perspective. There is no medication that will do this for you.
    I cry all the time. It makes the whites of my eyes very white. It's about controlled crying. It's about crying when you are in a safe place and crying as much as you need. I have cried for most of the day before. It's about draining your imbalances on your time. I do this by leaning into the emotions I feel until I cry it out. When I say lean in, I mean tell me what color it is, what does it smell like? What does the emotion feel like? Any words that evoke that emotion – write them down. I want you to become one with your emotion and feel it to your core. It might suck, but it's going to suck less than if you try to ignore it. There is a train of thought that if you do not process your emotions, they will get stuck in your body/organs. They can literally cause physical ailments in your body. People work with therapists to release these traumatic emotions from their body.
    Note that I cry for any intense emotion within me. I cry for happiness, for anger, for sadness, for excitement. Crying is how your body regulates neurotransmitters. While I try not to, I still cry in front of people all the time. I don't have an intense crying session, but my eyes tear up. Others notice, but I go on with my conversation. It's the passion within me and no one can make me feel like it is bad. Being emotional is a part of me and my reality; crying is not bad. Emotions are not bad. We need to understand this as a society – it's how one experiences the world. Crying is what I need sometimes to manage my emotions.

If you have the space, after a good cry, a nap/sleep is the next remedy. You will awaken in a better mood, guaranteed. No medication can do this for you. And it's completely free – you just need some time as every emotion is transient. If you struggle with sleeping, start with meditations. There are neurotransmitters that are released only when you sleep and/or meditate. Again, remember we are trying to combat these imbalances.

"Self-Acceptance of emotion = Success" (2018)
"How did you become successful?
I recall
Four years ago,
When you were a mess..."
Blessed
I guess
Is the best response on my chest.
You see, I cry!
All the time.
Letting the tears dry,
I find a release, one of a satisfying kind.
Clears up my red eye
Reminds me why
Release and saying bye
To those emotions when I cry
Is necessary for my mind.

In my hardest of times, I always revert to science to help me through the pain. I fundamentally believe that every person on this earth at this moment is a champion - a champion that has been refined after iterations of previous champions.

Nature is beautiful, and the best technology ever created is the body. The human body "updates" and refines itself like software, but better. The human body improves from mistakes until champions are made.

My life, just like yours, has been created after so many people reproduced through love affairs or magnetic attraction or destiny. So much pain, maybe famine and loss had to occur for any of us champions to be alive today.

<u>We matter and make an impact on our world daily. Survive through the temporary hard times, and conquer this, champion!</u>

CHAPTER FOUR:
MEDI-SIN OR MEDICINE?

"It's Medicine, not medi-SIN" (2017)
*Mystically indeed
Is how this weed
Helps me relieve
This pain...
Which won't refrain.
This monotony
Has gotten to me!
I need an expert in botany.
Because this herb
Can curb cancer!
Because this flower
Can power
Our mental evolution.
I doubt you have a better solution...
Because when chaos ensures,
It proves
To make me abuse
That plant with the green hues.
It's called medicine,
Not a contemporary sin
Not a recreational gin...
I even use it before the gym!
Weed
I need
As an OTC
To succeed
Indeed.
Medicine that I enjoy.
A subculture of acceptance and joy.*

I worked at a legal cannabis shop in San Diego, CA before it became legal recreationally. I even got my medical card for bipolar disorder, legally. I felt I had finally found the medicine I needed. I smoked every day, multiple times a day. I recall one of my doctors, Dr. Becker at Kaiser Permanente, would ask me every appointment if I smoked cannabis. I would tell him yes, and I remember him saying one time, "I just don't want you to get hooked on it." I didn't understand his concern until it was too late. He didn't want me smoking cannabis, but he also would say it was better than drinking alcohol (and I agree). I had a doctor tell me he would not treat me because I smoked cannabis. I had other doctors that told me I caused myself to "become bipolar" (whatever that means) by smoking cannabis. While others never even asked about my Cannabis Use Disorder (CUD as they call it in the medical literature).

The hardest thing for me is that mental health is still an art form – there were never conclusive studies that doctors could share with me about the negative/positive effects of cannabis. There were many studies, but the jury was still up on the concept in my opinion. This is one reason I kept self-medicating. It also really felt like it helped me sometimes. It would help me socialize and be in a predictable state of mind.

I wrote poems for the cannabis blog. I was a consumer of cannabis, and it was part of my identity and how I interacted with others. I felt like it was helping me. I felt that it would always put me in a predictable state of mind that I could not count on otherwise. It made me feel up when I was feeling down. It made my mind race a little, making me feel somewhat manic/"star power". I was deep into this addiction and was in denial that I needed help.

At my peak, I would spend from $200 to $400 a month on cannabis, while also receiving cannabis samples from work. I would love having people over to smoke them out.

I loved the way it made me think about interesting things and made me forget about the monotony of life. I made many friends through cannabis; living in California, it's easy to find others with this vice – and it's always nice to share vices with others (no matter how toxic, the community aspect makes it feel okay).

"Self-Prescribed" (2017)
I am in charge of my own prescription
Yes, I didn't stutter, that was my intentional diction.
The medical benefits of cannabis aren't fiction...
In fact, legal restrictions
On the herb, cause friction.
A substance that cannot become poison.
No documented ODs,
Caffeine, 20,000 Americans asking, "Get me an IV."
Who knows this?!
Self-prescribed for the desired effect
In this context,
I respect
that no one knows what they are doing.

    Now I know you should never confuse an addiction with medicine. Now that I am sober, I understand that if you are using any substance or activity for self-medication and to numb yourself, it's crucial to break through your denial and seek help. The act of abusing **anything** indicates an underlying issue that requires attention. In my case it was functional depression. I had a job; I paid my bills – I would justify my smoking. However, functionality doesn't necessarily equate to living your best life.
    I also want to emphasize that no one fully comprehends the intricacies of your brain chemistry. My advocacy lies in understanding how much you're consuming (dosage) and being honest with your support group about your usage. Cannabis can indeed be addictive, but the same applies to

other substances. I propose one to ask themselves this question - does the benefit of smoking outweigh the associated risks, given my current dosage and expense? Occasional cannabis use may be ok for most people, daily cannabis use should be avoided in my opinion.

The other substance of concern is alcohol. I believe alcohol should be avoided as often as possible. Abstaining from alcohol can be difficult because it's the only substance that people will ask you why you are not consuming – and make you feel out of place for it. Many times, my peers judged me for not drinking while at an event. They would ask if I was pregnant. "Why else would I not be drinking?" Also, it is difficult because it is almost everywhere, especially in California. The problem is that alcohol can wash away your issues and make you feel good, but at the end of the day, it's a depressant. In addition, it is counter indicated for most psychiatric medications. I think if you are going to abuse a drug, let it be cannabis not alcohol or hard drugs. Obviously, it's better to not abuse anything, but I understand the need to self-medicate. Ideally one would look for professional help, but even while receiving professional help, I abused cannabis and alcohol.

"Sober" (2019)
Opening my eyes
I can now see my prize.
I cannot deny
That I lived a lie
And just was alive for the high
A high that took me to lows
The low that really blows
The high that keeps me on the rise
Opening my eyes
I can now see my prize
In its actual size.

Sitting up high
Without any guys.
It's me.
As pure as can be.
It's me.
As healthy as I have seen.

    I talked to my least effective doctor about wanting to get pregnant. At that time, he had me on Lithium and Abilify. It's well-known that Lithium can lead to birth defects if taken during pregnancy. He mentioned I needed to be on Lithium indefinitely and refused to make any adjustments to my medications.

    I realized I needed to part ways with this doctor – he simply wasn't the right fit for me. I ended up taking a huge risk and going cold turkey off my medications and stopped seeing my doctor while I continued to work with my therapist and started doctor shopping. I was lucky that I did not spiral into mania and was able to keep my life stable "enough" during these couple months. I would not recommend replicating my actions, as I had intense withdrawals like chills, excessive sweating, irritability, and even cystic acne on my back.

    After a couple of months, I finally connected with a new psychiatrist who was recommended by my incredible therapist. This doctor, Dr. Sistov, changed the course of my life. By this time I've been seen by over ten doctors for my mental health, and I've rarely been impressed. But Dr. Sistov is an exception – he's truly brilliant.

    I entered his office unmedicated, feeling agitated and angry. He took the time to learn about me, my mental health history, the medications I'd tried, and the frustration I felt toward the medical system. He asked me, very empathetically, "Lauren, what advice would you offer someone like me, who is trying to assist you at this time?"

His question left me momentarily speechless – never had a doctor asked me something so profound. I conveyed my dissatisfaction with the mental healthcare system, highlighting its rapid growth and lack of concrete understanding. I told him, "No one really knows anything". [As a side note, perhaps my choice of words, "no one really knows anything," might come across as strong. However, the essence I aim to convey is that neuroscience, comprehension of the brain, and the mechanisms of medication action remain more of an art than a precise science. Some medications yield positive results for some individuals, while others don't, and many times, their effectiveness is observed without a clear understanding of why.]

I explained to him how I have had previous doctors, some of whom were truly subpar. I shared my frustration over a doctor who prescribed me an SSRI (known to trigger mania) and then shifted to administrative work, leaving me to navigate withdrawal under the care of a new psychiatrist. I also ranted about another doctor who provided me with medication samples after just one 10-minute appointment. By that point in my psychiatric journey, I had decided to stop experimenting with new medications. I had come to realize that while pharmaceutical companies excel at getting doctors to prescribe their medications, they don't conduct studies on how it feels to discontinue them. In addition, the clinical trails are not as robust as one would expect. In the case of Vraylar , the FDA approval involved a three-week study for a class of medication that takes two weeks to take full effect in the bloodstream. That limited data was all the FDA needed to approve its effectiveness for my condition.

"Vraylar" (2018)
Clinical Studies lasting three weeks.
Call my outlook bleak,

> *But I can't even speak…*
> *Because the money grubbing is at its peak.*
> *Pharma companies making profits that are steep!*
> *Creating a pill to be taken 7 days a week*
> *Until you become peat*
> *You think, in the end, big pharma will take the heat?*

Recall that these medications are prescribed for daily use (and often for life). I felt this was preposterous, but it's the reality of medications for mental illness – there isn't much long-term data on newer medications inherently, and the FDA approves them with studies that effectively last one week. How is this possible? It's simple, the standard that the FDA uses to approve the safety and effectiveness of all medications is "benefit outweighs risk." Thus, in the case of Vraylar and others, the FDA sees that the risk of taking the medication is less than the benefit it would provide for bipolar disorder episodes. These concepts, the fact that there are no studies about suspending psychiatric medications, and the subjective FDA assessment of "benefit outweighs risk," should be considered any time you decide to go on a new medication. Ask questions, look at the studies, understand what it means for you specifically. Be empowered. This is your life; be an advocate for yourself and learn about the medications you are prescribed. Read your packet inserts. **Do not take medications blindly.** Read the side effects, the studies, the drug interactions – these are serious medications!

"Uhhhhh-Merican Pharmaceuticals" (2015)
> *They are taking our diagnosis*
> *And creating a money oasis*
> *The market for daily pharmaceuticals*
> *Keeps us drugged*
> *But are these pills suitable*
> *For long-term human consumption?*

Dependency and potential for abuse is a function
Of its chemical components...
The FDA pretends they know this.
Schedule 1, too much fun
Schedule 2, I guess it's ok for you!
Creating legal addicts every day
Dependent on big pharma in every way.
Looking to make the next wonder drug,
But if it doesn't make money,
We don't give a flying fuck!

After going on a rant about my terrible experiences with medications and psychiatrists, Dr. Sistov said something else to me: "Lauren, I am your placebo effect, I need you to believe in me and the treatment and, if nothing else, the placebo effect will work; I could be selling sugar pills in some cases, you need to believe." The amazing thing about this statement was that he is right. Even in Clinical Trials, you will notice that the placebo effect sometimes has up to a 15% effectiveness. How amazing is this! The mind's ability to heal our bodies when it thinks it can heal is amazing and should not go unnoticed. Just like kids believe in Santa, you must believe in the treatment you are receiving from your doctor. After Dr. Sistov listened to me empathetically (something I wasn't used to), I brought my defenses down and was ready to get help. He prescribed my Abilify monotherapy to help with my mania, and we discussed a newer treatment called Transcranial Magnetic Stimulation (TMS) as a potential add-on for the future if I suffered from the depressive sides of the disorder. Months go by and I continue to abuse cannabis and take my Abilify, but life was still grey. It was the beginning of April 2021 when I realized that I needed more help. I was a highly functioning depressed person. I would work, smoke, sleep, and repeat. Many times, I would be asleep by 5:30 PM, right after work because I just wanted the day to end. I realized that it was a necessity for me to get help because I will be alone with these thoughts for the rest of my life if I didn't.

I met back with Dr. Sistov, and we decided to start an experimental TMS treatment for depression. I didn't have anything to lose and everything to gain. This was the turning point for me. I changed my "I should take care of my mind" into an "I have to take care of my mind." In the month of April (2021), I scheduled my TMS treatment, I stopped smoking weed, and I started working out with a trainer who gave me a diet plan. All I had in my mind was a belief that I could be better. A dream that I could be better. The affirmation I kept repeating was "I am conquering my illness." I quit weed on 4/20/2021 – the national weed-smoking day. This was not easy, I learned one thing about quitting bad habits – it's almost impossible. You don't want to focus on quitting a bad habit; you want to focus your energy on starting a new one. Therefore, I took drastic measures in April. My goal was to get help for my depression and quit my addiction – for good. Instead of work, smoke, sleep, I was replacing it with a workout, work, workout, sleep. I started meal prepping and focusing on eating clean; I started working out twice a day.

Six days after the start of my brave lifestyle changes, I started my TMS protocol. It was April 26th when I started my first TMS treatment. Karla was my technician, and I was very nervous, especially after signing the waivers that this was an experimental treatment. Dr. Sistov comes in, and Karla proceeded to determine the threshold. They zapped me until my right hand started twitching. I just about lost it; I did not like this feeling. I find out it's just to determine the starting strength for the stimulation. I calmed down and proceeded with the treatment. My treatment was two 10-minute sessions (45 minutes apart) of TMS for five consecutive days. After the first day, I went home and cleaned my house. I felt motivated, clear, happy, like the clouds had passed.

During the treatment, they placed a machine on your head and it felt as if you had some bugs in your hair... that were scratching your scalp. I got a headache for one of the treatments, but it subsided a couple of hours after the treatment. No other side effects! What a miraculous treatment! It was a complete success. I don't like to say things are magic, but TMS is like a miracle that I didn't know I needed. In the month of April, I got a revolutionary treatment to help balance my functional depression, started working out, and stopped smoking weed. It was time to be brave, and I am glad I did. It is scary to change, but change is the only constant. I think I was able to quit cannabis, happily, because the TMS treatment treated my underlying depression that I was attempting to self-medicating. In addition, filling my time with a productive fitness habit also benefited me. After my last 4/20 smoke sesh, I knew that cannabis was not my identity any longer. I had cut the cords of self-denial that sought help. Self-medicating is a true indicator that you need help – don't be afraid to ask for help. A miracle could be coming if you just ask for help.

"Content" (May 2021)
I feel content. I feel at home in my skin.
More importantly, my mind.
Of confine... of love.
Silence is loud.
But like music loud.
Like I want to listen to it more.
Thank you.
In my mind I find a kind

CHAPTER FIVE:
DEFINE IT WITH GRACE

"ABOVE" (2019)
You see, you see.
This bipolarity,
It's in me.
This abnormality
Will allow me
To change the world –
Not linearly –
EXPONENTIALLY –
Not chronologically,
I am here to change society.
Remember, the opposite of down,
Is ABOVE.

People always think that bipolar people are "up" or "down". I strive to be "above" - "above the stigma", "above the statistics," and "above the prognosis." Don't let your diagnosis define you and your unique journey; decide to define it. Let the diagnosis do what it is supposed to do – help the healing process. You don't define a person by their cancer diagnosis; let's not define ourselves by any medical diagnosis. Medical diagnoses are meant to help you get help and, as my therapist says, "get reimbursed by insurance." The problem with healthcare for bipolar patients is that stigma is rampant, even among medical professionals. Societal, self-induced, and caregivers' stigmas all are a reality that keeps people from getting help.

You would think that mentally ill patients are given equal access to programs, or there are measures to avoid discrimination, but this is not the case with Bipolar disorder. A couple of things that you cannot do with a

Bipolar diagnosis are 1) serve in the military, 2) get mortgage insurance 3) get short-term or long-term disability insurance. I looked into the military once when I learned they screened for mental illness. I personally wasn't too upset with this result, but I do think it's a type of discrimination. If this disorder is manageable with doctors and medication, why couldn't I serve in non-combat types of roles? For me, I was happy that I found my career in healthcare instead of the military. I was also denied mortgage insurance and short-term/long-term disability insurance. This is more of an issue to me, considering that people with mental illness are most at risk for disability or needing assistance with their mortgage. I don't believe it's right to use a medical diagnosis (that can be managed) to exclude people from programs. I accepted the loss on these insurance denials, but I do think it's a type of discrimination.

 I remember when I was first diagnosed, I was told by many people, not to tell anyone that I was bipolar due to the stigma I would receive. I went about my life trying to keep my trauma to myself, but then I realized that the only way I could be part of the solution to decrease stigma would be to talk about it, to let people know what bipolar is and what it is like to live with it. I decided instead of letting it define me, I am going to be part of the force to define it, and I hope you will help me, too. Instead of being afraid of the judgments, I was going to let them relate to me, love me for who I am, and then drop in the "oh yeah, and I am bipolar." I call it "relating and educating." This helps me define what it means to be bipolar, instead of it defining me. Since I was diagnosed, I figured out that the three most stigmatized groups of people are 1) mentally ill 2) homeless, and 3) addicts. In addition, about a quarter of all people killed by the police are mentally ill (2). Patients have even been killed in hospitals by police officers. This could have been **me**. What is terrifying for me is that

mental illness can be in all three of these categories. Since 2010, I have studied stigma and how to remove it, and "relating and educating" was the tactic I devised that would de-stigmatize bipolar in the most effective way, a personal relationship by personal relationship.

I have learned that the only way to decrease stigma is empathy. People lack empathy for bipolar patients because many people create dissonance in their minds about how a mentally ill person acts when compared to "normal" people. Also, many don't know who is bipolar and use Hollywood and the media's depiction of bipolar as a guide. Thus, "normal" people many times see two buckets, people like me ("normal" people) and people not like me (mentally ill people). When you create a divide like this in your mind about who is and isn't like you, you feel okay about judging, stereotyping, and removing rights from stigmatized people. I was actively out to break this cycle by allowing people to relate and empathize with me, and then educating them about my diagnosis; this way, they would have empathy for me as a person and it would be more difficult for the stigma to overtake their judgments. The funny thing is that people always respond with, "I had no idea you were bipolar." This gives me joy because this reaction indicates to me that I have done a good job of generating surprise within them; my favorite emotion to evoke because it is normally followed by additional contemplation. Contemplation being what we need to reduce stigma.

I think that being vulnerable about my diagnosis has helped many "normal" people realize that mentally ill people are people too and that it can be debilitating, scary, and very traumatic. Thus, I like to think I am ABOVE the stigma because I accept my diagnosis and talk about bipolar disorder and ask for help when needed. I am ABOVE the statistics because I pledge to not self-destruct and become just another suicide statistic. I am ABOVE the prognosis because I dare to dream and make my life goals into a reality. Being ABOVE bipolar disorder is not easy, but it is a necessity if you want to live your dream. Nothing that is worthwhile is easy, but that is why you need to have your "Why," your daring dream to ground you in difficult times. I listen to motivational speeches often, and many people talk about the "why" behind their goals as a concept. You must take this "normal" people's "why" and raise it to the next level. Remember, everyone is bipolar with ups and downs; the "why" is needed for everyone to help manage these fluctuations. If you are bipolar, your "why" has to, like your emotional ranges, be stronger and more defined than the "normal" person next to you. This doesn't sound fair, but life isn't fair. It's a daily challenge, an opportunity to prioritize ones' thoughts and align ones' atoms to one goal, and to make ones "why" a must-do/must-have.

    Bipolar disorder is debilitating and changes your entire life and relationships. It is a disorder that needs treatment to live a good life and survive this life. It can be easy to look at your prognosis and the statistics and be overwhelmed. It happened to me. But there comes a moment when you must decide what you want your life to be like. Do you want to fall into the cycles, statistics, and emotional pain prescribed with your diagnosis? Or do you want to create standards for yourself and a dream to keep you stable and focused? People have been bipolar for years. There have been millions of diagnosed bipolar patients, and there are trends that occur with this disorder, just like there are trends that occur with cancer and diabetes. The only way you are going to be able to define your bipolar journey is by learning about your disorder from your doctors and others with the disorder. Take your medication. Do therapy. Love and thank your support network. Dream. Cry. Sleep. Eat well. Pledge to seek help and not self-destruct. You can define your life, regardless of your diagnosis – it might just take a little more effort than others, but it's worth it!

> ***"Bipolar I AM" (2020)***
> *As Lauren Gann, I stand*
> *Until all can understand*
> *That I am not bland*
> *Creativity is a part of me*
> *Entropy of the mind can be*
> *DESTRUCTIVE.*
> *But I am a creator*
> *CONSTRUCTIVE,*
> *Productive!*
> *I live for creativity!*

Today is the present because it is a gift. It's essential to think of the world this way because it provides a grateful perspective, and when you are flowing in the present, the future falls into place. Sometimes it feels like today presently gave us a terrible attitude, a negative perspective, and complaints/excuses. It happens. But don't let it happen for long. I am not saying you must go from angry because you missed the promotion to happy like a little kid at a petting zoo; I am saying identify your present emotion and just progress to a happier mood. It may be that you were in rage and now you are just angry – that is progress. Maybe it's that you were hopeless and now you are numb. Be graceful of your progress in life and with your moods. Understand what makes you happier. What makes you smile when your face muscles are frowning? What makes you laugh when you are raging with anger? Do that! Be gentle with your journey to be happier; it takes a lot of self-reflection and emotional intelligence. Know that progress is important for happiness, and progress is not linear! Once you stop progressing, you will struggle with happiness. Happiness is not a destination but a **side effect of progress**.

I feel like I progress in cycles that many times start with destruction and rebuilding.

>**"You don't know the future" (2020)**
>*It's pure*
>*Mystery.*
>*You don't know the past,*
>*You pull it out of your ass.*
>*You don't know the present,*
>*Because you are too busy lamenting*
>*The former.*
>*But you live in the present day.*
>*You hesitate*
>*And complicate*
>*The equation*
>*By looking beyond your control*
>*....*
>*Which makes you lose control.*
>*You can only control the now.*
>*How*
>*Can we*
>*POWOW*
>*On this concept?*
>*It will make the world happier.*
>*Sounds sappy, but that's what we need in 2020.*

I am a professional at rebuilding, as I have "destroyed" my life three times – once every manic episode. I ended up with no money, debt, no job, wrecked relationships. I have rebuilt with new jobs, new relationships, and new saving techniques. I was only able to do this because I gave myself grace and focused my energy not on being self-deprecating, but on rebuilding.

>*Backwards (2022)*
>*Backward, I start for a fresh outlook...*

*Backward is forward when you have undergone the
destruction I have created.
I am accountable.
I am rebuilding.
I will generate the best life possible –
Better than I could imagine.
Because from destruction and fire
Comes rebirth.
Thank you, universe, for this opportunity to rebuild.
Forward I will go. In a backward way.*

    I didn't look backward, I only looked forward. Even though my episodes were awful, and I would never want to relive them, the destruction that occurred during these episodes helped me create a better life for me at the end of the day. The first episode kept me out of graduate school debt and made me land my first job at a medical software company, which launched my fruitful career. My second episode got me out of a job I hated. My third episode got me out of a toxic relationship and helped me land my highest-paying job. Destruction can lead to building a better foundation - if the destruction does not tear down your hope and forward movement.
    The grace I have given myself is the fundamental trait that has allowed me to rebuild. I understand I have a mental illness that I cannot control and did not decide to have. I know that I am doing the best I can to care for myself, and sometimes that isn't enough, and I need help. Energy is finite; the more you can focus on moving forward, the better your life will turn out. Do not waste energy on criticizing yourself. I could spend all my energy on criticizing my decisions and actions during my manic episodes, but I don't – for my own good. Apologize to those whom you may have hurt. Apologize to yourself for stopping your medication and not caring for yourself. Think about what you can do today; think about where you

can go tomorrow. Yesterday's mood/episode is behind you – learn from it, and don't let it hold you back from your best life.

"My hobby" (2021)
Witness the range of frequencies
Ready to change future histories...
Bipolar brain waves,
It's not a conspiracy,
But seriously...
Misunderstood.
My brain waves need words
To extinguish
my moods.
Y'all will peruse
My nonfiction
while my rhymes
Create friction
In corpus colosseums...
No addiction
Can create the neural
Conditions
That my words produce...
Not even a meth kitchen.
Evolution is kicking
In the neural networks, I am picking
Through thought.
Making you think more
Is how I keep score.
Bringing juncture
To thought pathways,
My goal, always.

What do I do with all my emotions, though? Have grace and create art! Art is present across cultures as a means of sharing emotions, tapping into our shared emotional essence. Energy is neither created nor destroyed; it transforms. Emotions are energy! Art transforms emotional energy from one to many. I feel an emotion, it inspires a poem, which touches 4 people – my emotional energy now lives in them. Mental illness can enhance creativity – learn to express yourself in productive, beautiful ways. If bipolar disorder lacked utility, it wouldn't have endured natural selection. I believe its utility lies in art and creativity. Select an outlet that lets you escape and embrace emotion – painting, photography, and beyond. Your mode of expression needn't be words. It's about giving shape (color, form) to emotions. Imagine externalizing emotions, shaping them in your mind, and channeling them into evocative art.

With more emotions, comes more energy, especially in the arts. A sad individual paints chilling scenes, an elevated mood can create a new perspective in a sculpture. Channel this energy for good – make it extraordinary! When channeled, abundant emotions yield incredible achievements.

Start by identifying and being emotionally aware. What's the emotion? Can you handle it alone or need professional help? If you pay attention, every emotion has distinct features – color, size, weight, shape, location. Crucially, you need to determine if your emotion is positive or not? Once identified, transform it. Redirect emotion into something constructive. My outlet is writing. Organizing feelings, perhaps rhyming, lets me release emotion, and triggers thought in others.

Having grace and creating art helps me be the best I can be as often as possible because it releases energy within me. It lets me process my emotions and bottle them up for later (or never). This is part of being crazy good – being able to extinguish the emotion to live a better life.

"Emotional" (2019)
Commotional.

Uncontrollable?
NO! I am capable.
I have been given ample
Time to sample
EMOTIONS;
Taste EMOTIONS;
Smell, feel, and hear
EMOTIONS.
<u>I digest emotions</u>
<u>And it fuels me.</u>
Therefore, you see…
*I have **more** energy;*
***More** life to create synergy!*

CHAPTER SIX:
I AM CRAZY GOOD.

    Bipolar is a mood disorder, not a personality disorder, and not an excuse for bad behavior or a pass on bad behavior. While hallucinations and mania can cause you to make questionable decisions, you are still accountable for your decisions. There is no magic wand that removes responsibility from you. You will still need to apologize to people you may have wronged, and you will still need to pay for medical bills; you do not get a free pass. In addition, you can be a stable bipolar patient who is a jerk and a liar. You can be stable and steal and assault people. Stability is just a foundation to show your true colors. One should ensure they keep this in mind – you still need to work on your personality and how you treat people once you are stable, just like everyone else. Being crazy good is working on your stability so you can then build your character and individuality on a stable foundation so you can become the best person you are capable of being. If you struggle with finances and drug abuse, getting stable is still the first step, but there any many more steps to conquer. We have to get stable and then start the self development to become a great person.

    One technique I use to help me be the best I can, as often as possible, is writing and saying mantras and affirmations. Affirmations are short "I am" statements, like "I am crazy good." "I am destined for greatness". "I am conquering my illness," ...just to name a few of my favorites. These are great to write out in your journal and to say them out loud until you internalize them. They can influence your confidence and your chakras (energy centers in your spine). Mantras are anything you say repeatedly. An affirmation can also be a mantra. I have had the mantra

"I will conquer this" since 2009, but below is an example of a longer mantra I wrote after my third episode:

> *No person is more equipped and more able to be healthy, mentally, spiritually, and physically than me. The past will not be repeated because I am wiser, more aware, with clear pragmatic analytical tools to execute my intention: peace of mind and physical health. I will not give my power away by allowing external factors to influence my state of calmness. My peace of mind was created by me, it will be maintained by me, and it will be the key to channeling my immense energy and power for my larger goals.*

I recommend mantras and affirmations to be handwritten and spoken aloud as it makes it more effective, I have found. You can even record yourself and listen to it daily – a technique I learned from a life coaching training. It deals with neuroplasticity and neurolinguistic programming. Something about seeing your own handwriting or hearing your own voice saying something positive about yourself will really resonate with you and has been shown to help manifest your reality.

This chapter contains some more of my poetry, my art that allows me to be sane and create for the world. It helps me be crazy good because it is my outlet for emotion. Find out what your "crazy good" is and let's define mental health and make the world happier. Have grace in knowing that sometimes you cannot be 100% because bipolar disorder is a disability; just be the best that you can, as often as possible. Conquer your disorder not once, but daily. Use mantras and affirmations to keep your energy high. Do not judge yourself for things you cannot control – like your diagnosis. Let's be crazy good and define bipolar disorder together!

"Lower than sea level" (2022)
I am in the mantle of the earth's crust.
I am a crust…
If bread
Undesired
But necessary
Only consumed by some.
My pain is dull.
My energy is… meh…
My desire is numb.
It's official - I am depressed.
Talking is too difficult.
It expends all of my energy.
One day, not today, I will look back at this and say, this was easy.
I will talk about this as if it was a walk in the park.

Until then, the pain runs through me in a dull but consistent fashion.
The kind of pain you don't even realize hurts until it's gone.
I am misunderstood by myself.
I am mistreated by myself.
I look to new beginnings
Because the past is futile.
The past is fake - it's either a fake iteration of positivity or a dull reminder of my limitations.
But as I age, I remind myself that I am destined for greatness.
As the moments pass, I know I have a purple, and that purpose is like that of a bread crust.
To be consumed and enjoyed by limited people as I represent the boundary that I need to create for myself from our malevolent world. I will conquer this.

"The battle to get out of the haze" (2017)
In these days
All I do is blaze
Until the numbness stays
Until it sprays
On all the gays

I mean happy people,
Whatever, gets off your steeple.
And quite with your labels
That perpetuate fables

Medicalization -
The new discourse;
Ready to fuck us and call it intercourse.
Politically correct,
This discourse coming at me fully erect

Entrusted by most,
And even included in toasts,
But this haze
Of today's
Is stronger than me.

These meds aren't medicine
This label is a sin
Today I battled and lost
But right now begins the war.

"Masticated by Mania" (2022)
I rest my head as it depresses into my pillow.
Not just physically depresses, but emotionally
Not just emotionally depresses, but spiritually.

I close my eyes and feel relief.
I sleep like it's medicine
I sleep like it's an addiction
I sleep because it's death to reality.
Death to depression.

Sedated by depression,
I can't with my sleep cycles,
They have me jaded.
Complicated, but I feel reincarnated;
Reincarnated
But sedated
With depression.
Had to shed old skin because mania masticated me.

I am a new person, after episode three,
Unable to look back, pretending to be free from this inconsistency...
Persistently, I progress.
Forward because backward doesn't produce success.
Forward, I focus because the universe says "hocus pocus"
Manifesting for me a reality that I could hardly conceive

"Smoke Sesh Healing"
Pain doesn't know your skin color.
Insomnia doesn't know your religion.
My mood doesn't know I am a woman.
But please, people, come over and listen.
We all suffer from something,
No one's genetics are perfect,
Some people have their own judgments
But relating over cannabis helps disseminate this
This weed is a special medicine that unites.
Unites all of us into one room,

To talk about our medication.
One of us is full of hesitation,
He has never been high! Good gracious!
Stoner culture is there to help and make ya comfortable
No one asks why, we are just getting high.
Suddenly my diagnosis doesn't matter,
My pain subsides
And I find a kind
Of comfort.
Who is one to say this cannabis subculture
Isn't it part of the healing process?
Support groups not sounding appealing, but relating with
thy fella stoner, I'll be there swiftly.

"This void" 2020
A frown in a Polaroid,
Feels like it's on steroids.
This void
Is a lack of action
And thus reaction.
This hole is a lack of filling
Which has kept me "chilling"....

It's time to change the game
Cuz "chilling" isn't getting me fame-
I want fame, but Not in vain
But for those in pain
I want to leave a stain
On their membrane
To help them reclaim
Their brain.

"Grace" (2022)
It took so many love affairs to create me.
It took so much despair...and care...to make me. It took me
and others so much to make the person I am today...

*Thus, I won't let myself lose my identity again. Thus, I
won't misplace my identity tomorrow.
I am Lauren Gann, and I have a purpose.
I am Lauren Gann...and no pain will make me refrain from
the gains that the world is yet to contain. Because the pain
make me stronger. Because the strength I have is
unbelievable...So unmeasurable, I cannot even fathom it,
because I have taken it for granted.
So today, I grant myself grace.
Grace to face the world that's INSANE...
Because...I will conquer this.*

"Insane" (2022)
*Is my brain....
Locked in invisible chains.
Insane.
Did you call my name?
Because I can't proclaim
What my heart feels today.*

"A mind with mind tricks" (2022)
*Sometimes, all I want is nothing.
Sometimes, nothing is what I do.
I start but don't finish.
I am passionate but terrified.
I am not meant for mediocre,
But I experience phases of emotion in life.
I am not ok with negative judgment,
But, not ok with telling myself a lie.
I write to inspire.
I cry to the world in sheer love for existence...
I see the world as a miracle....
Everything I search for - I decide is not my destiny.
I am a lost soul -*

With a mind that plays tricks on her.
As the days go by, I value silence.
I value peace, subtle murmurs... love.

"Depressed state" (2021)
It's part of my oppressed fate.
Self-hate.
I have this feeling to date.
No mate
Will remove this complication
that occurs in the bipolar nation.
Totaling 2.3 million today!
This depressive iteration
Of reality creates a complicated
Emotional compilation.
The juxtaposition of the two conditions
Makes survival less auspicious.
I don't have a good solution; depressive thoughts are pollution.
It's no collusion
That depression
KILLS.

Paralyze me, please!
I need to be paralyzed by this negative emotion
So I don't overanalyze and act on my
Mental commotion.
I lean into the pain...
Knowing I am not completely sane....
Every emotion is transient
I pause my actions
So I don't regret my reactions to my depressed state. I will conquer this.

BIBLIOGRAPHY:

Novick, D. M., Swartz, H. A., & Frank, E. (2010). Suicide attempts in bipolar I and bipolar II disorder: a review and meta-analysis of the evidence. *Bipolar disorders*, *12*(1), 1-9.

Stout, C. (2018). How mental illness affects police shooting fatalities. *International Bipolar Foundation. Retrieved June*, *15*, 2021.

Made in the USA
Columbia, SC
15 February 2025

53842720R00039